# Lost in Time

## GOD'S GRACE IN THE MIDST OF DEMENTIA

## Diane Bentley

TRILOGY CHRISTIAN PUBLISHERS

*TUSTIN, CA*

Trilogy Christian Publishers
A Wholly Owned Subsidary of Trinity Broadcasting Network
2442 Michelle Drive
Tustin, CA 92780

For information, address Trilogy Christian Publishing

Rights Department, 2442 Michelle Drive, Tustin, Ca 92780.

Trilogy Christian Publishing/ TBN and colophon are trademarks of Trinity Broadcasting Network.

For information about special discounts for bulk purchases, please contact Trilogy Christian Publishing.

Manufactured in the United States of America

10 9 8 7 6 5 4 3 2 1

Library of Congress Cataloging-in-Publication Data is available.

ISBN 978-1-64773-334-6

ISBN 978-1-64773-335-3

# Contents

# Preface

As challenging as caregiving can be, I cannot fathom being unable to be there. To those individuals who are and were unable to be with their loved ones during the COVID-19 pandemic:

Some survived, but loved ones were unable to be with them during the illness.

Some did not survive, and loved ones were unable to be with them during their illness nor as they passed.

Some were residents of long-term care facilities and loved ones were unable to visit.

Some lost to COVID-19 or other illnesses could not be celebrated by loved ones at the time.

Dads could not be there with moms and babies during birth.

Healthcare workers, frontline witnesses to the devastation, avoided being with their families to protect them.

May the Lord bless and keep each of you in His perfect peace.

DIANE BENTLEY

# Prologue

This book is a revelation of God's grace in my life during a challenging time. It is a struggle that it seems is becoming so much more prevalent in many families. And I feel sure there are very few people who either have not experienced it or have known someone who has. It is facing the challenges of caring for a loved one with dementia.

I speak of many family members involved, and family dynamics vary. So, I should provide my own dynamics. I am one of five children, and my parents divorced in the early 1980s.

When I was eleven years old, my youngest brother, Kevin, was born with Down syndrome. Though my dad worked long hours in a job that was physically demanding during the week, he enjoyed being outside on weekends. He loved gardening and working in the yard, and on weekends, Kevin was my dad's shadow, doing everything with him during those times. Inevitably, when my dad retired, Kevin chose to go live with him. It was just the two of them in the home.

Kevin was the center of attention in our home when we were growing up. Kevin was nine years younger than my next youngest brother, and he had everyone to care for him. He still enjoys being the center of attention!

I always say that Kevin has taught me so much more than I could ever teach him. He has truly been a tremendous blessing in our lives. However, when you make someone the center of attention in your home... they tend to develop the mentality that regardless of where they are, or the circumstances, the world revolves around them! Kevin was no exception. Life to him is a big continuous PARTY! He is continuously looking for a reason to celebrate and plan a party. He is also very good at delegating the actual work for the party to others! I tell him he needs a job as a party planner!

My dad, especially, treated Kevin as though the world revolved around him. He wanted to provide anything and everything that Kevin wanted. He wanted to take him anywhere he wanted to go, do anything he wanted to do, and buy him anything he wanted to buy! If it was possible, my dad did it for Kevin. His plan was that when he retired, he and Kevin would travel and have fun—you know, the continuous party Kevin loves so much!

However, within a short time after my dad retired, he developed health problems and became less active. And actually...some of his health problems began prior to retirement. As a result, he was unable to do everything he had planned with Kevin, but he still provided a lot of fun for him.

I also have a sister, who lives five or six hours away, and another brother who was living over an hour away during my dad's illness. He was also serving in full time ministry at that time. I have another brother who, due to his own impairment, was unable to be responsible for my dad.

My dad was one of twelve children, which included seven brothers and five sisters. He had already lost multiple brothers at the time of his diagnosis, and he lost another during his illness. However, his sisters and one brother were living nearby and were able to assist in some ways with his care. They are very attentive to each other's needs.

I am married to Dennis, without whom I am sure I would never have been able to do all that I did. He was such an amazing support, and he did so much for my dad and his own parents, as well. I am so thankful for his love and care during this season of our lives.

Dennis and I have two amazing sons who have been willing to help out as much as possible with our parents.

My oldest son, Joshua, has done things for our parents that I never expected a young man in his early twenties would do for them. My youngest, Austin, has helped in other ways, which is also deeply appreciated. I am so thankful for my family and their support. I wholeheartedly believe that this period of time would have been so much more difficult without them. I am truly blessed!

The care and concern shown to me by my children during this time, in addition to their care for our parents, also extends beyond what words can express. They watched as I took on the primary role in my dad's care and as we cared for my in-laws at various times. They wanted to be there for us as best they could, and they were! Thank you so much for being the amazing sons you are! And thank you, Dennis, for having my back!

I speak most freely about my main and most consistent support during this time, my most precious heavenly Father. Without His love, wisdom, grace, and mercies, I could not have done this. I do not know how people go through this life without Him. He is my rock and my strong tower. He is my shelter, my shield, and the lifter of my head! When you are traveling this road of life and encounter this or any other difficult circumstance, I pray that He is your rock, as well. To Him I give all praise, honor, and glory for anything good that comes from my life—and from this book!

# Diagnosis: Answer or More Questions?

It was November 2005, and my dad was seeing a neurologist due to a referral by his cardiologist. He had developed some tremors in his hands, which the cardiologist had observed during a follow-up visit after treatment for a blockage. He had also had two hospital visits due to excessive bleeding related to medications prescribed following the procedure for the blockage. I had tried to explain away the tremor, as well as some behaviors I had observed, as being related to weakness due to the blockage and bleeding. Dad also tried really hard to conceal it, and it could have been occurring for a long period of time without others noticing. He would often place his hands in his pockets, and he later told me that helped him to control the tremor.

I recalled an incident the day he was discharged from the hospital after the second admission due to bleeding. It was a Friday, and my brother Kevin, who has Down syndrome, wanted to go to the local high school football game. Though I was sure my father should not attempt this, he insisted. As I previously mentioned, his life and world revolved around Kevin and what Kevin wanted. I was concerned about taking the two of them to the game due to my dad's weakness. But I was concerned that if I did not agree to take them, my dad might try to drive them to the game himself, and I felt he was in no condition to do this.

So I agreed to take them, and when the ballgame was over, I recall that as my dad got up to leave the stadium, a gentleman and his daughter were in front of us talking as they walked out. The crowd was moving slowly, and my dad began to jab this gentleman in the back, saying something like, "People need to wait until they get out of the stands to talk so we can get out!" The tone in his voice was somewhat hostile, and I was in shock—speechless that he was not only so rude, but also was so physically aggressive toward the man, as well! Had my chin dropped much farther, I am sure it would have hit the ground!

As soon as we were out of the stands, I told my dad I needed to find my husband, Dennis. I began to walk away from Dad and Kevin, then jog, then run (which for me is probably more like a jog). When I found Dennis, I told him we had to get out of there. He asked what was wrong, and I told him we just had to get out of there. As we walked out into the parking lot, I froze and became very alarmed again because I realized I had left Kevin with my dad and I was not sure what was going on with him. However, I did not go back, and finding them in the crowd before they got to the car likely would have been challenging, if not impossible anyway.

I remember going home and wondering over the entire weekend... *Does he have Alzheimer's? Is he just so weak that he had no patience with that man?* I had also observed some memory issues or confusion in him...but could that not be related to his recent illness, as well? He did seem to improve at times, and the symptoms were not consistently visible.

And yet...here we were. I sat with my dad in the office of a neurologist, awaiting the second most dreaded words I had ever heard in my life. The most dreaded had been when my mother told me she was divorcing my father. There are sometimes announcements or declarations in this life that we hope to never hear. Although we know others hear them, we want to believe... to hope...that we never will. Yet we are not promised a life without pain and suffering, and we will not avoid it in this broken and fallen world.

And as I listened, they came...those dreaded words. The neurologist stated that my dad had either Alzheimer's disease and Parkinson's disease *or* Lewy body dementia, which is a combination of Alzheimer's-type dementia and parkinsonism. The neurologist explained that the only way to be certain which diagnosis was accurate would be through an autopsy. Some types of testing were just not possible due to my dad's pacemaker and stints, but they might not have made the diagnosis more definitive anyway. Other testing, a neuropsychological test, has now become the standard for diagnosis of various types of dementia, I am told. But I am not certain if that test was being used at that time.

The neurologist explained that the treatment options were basically the same for either diagnosis. However, these common forms of treatment were sometimes less effective for Lewy body dementia than for the separate diagnoses of Alzheimer's and Parkinson's diseases. He prescribed medication for both the dementia and the Parkinson's symptoms, and he requested to see Dad again in three months.

As we left the doctor's office, it became clear that my father did not believe the neurologist. He never liked that doctor...it was not personal...the doctor was telling him something he did not want to hear. How often do we shrug off a word from God or someone through whom He has chosen to speak to give us a word because it is not what we want to hear? My dad did not want to go back to that neurologist, and he tried to convince either me, or himself, or maybe both of us, that this doctor was not accurate, and he should not be seeing him. We so often try to avoid what is difficult to see or hear, yet sometimes it can be so very much what we need.

Obtaining this answer, though it was not what I would have hoped for or thought I needed, did give me direction. Because I am a thinker and a planner, immediately following the dreaded task of informing my siblings as well as my dad's siblings of the diagnosis, I began my research. I found that, although we had been given an answer for the things we were seeing, I had so many more questions than answers. There were so many unknowns, and I was so uncertain of what would lie ahead. I am certain that no one person's experience or perspective is exactly the same as another person's. However, talking to others who shared this experience gave me the support I needed, just in knowing that someone else understood what I was going through. I still had so many questions, and this was new and uncharted territory. I had to prepare myself.

My dad had been a very independent person, and he did not easily open himself up to others for help. He always wanted to be the one providing help for others, not the one receiving it. I can be so much like him in that respect, as can other family members. Let's just say I got a double dose of it with my parents! However, as a child of God, I have learned that I desperately need to be on the receiving end of His help! That has enabled me to be more receptive to help from other people. Also, as I get older, I seem to feel the need for more help! But not so for my dad! When we did eventually bring other support into his home, he agreed only as long as it was helping the support person.

My dad and I also shared the introverted, analytical thinker personality type. We both spend so much more time thinking and overanalyzing than we do engaging with others. It can be very difficult to know what he is thinking and how he is responding to circumstances and others. How would he ever be receptive to the help he would eventually need? I will say, however, the dementia appeared to eventually remove any barriers that prevented him from expressing his thoughts and feelings about things. That is enough said about that for now!

Many questions flooded my thoughts regarding my dad and this horrific illness. How long would it be

LOST IN TIME

safe for him to drive? How long would he be able to live alone, especially with Kevin, who would not be able to be responsible for him? How long would he...could he live with this illness? How long would it be until he no longer knew me? How long?

My mind then took me to my areas of concern for my dad's emotional and spiritual well-being. Because he was an introverted thinker, he did not often speak of personal things, including spirituality. Possibly, because we shared those introverted and private traits, those discussions rarely occurred between us anyway. He was not always faithful to a church. I recall that while I was growing up, he did not attend with us, but sometimes that was due to his job, right? He told me once that he remembers me crying and pleading with him to go to church with us when I was young. I did not recall him attending faithfully until after my parents divorced. And yet, he did understand very well that believers were called to care for the fatherless and the widows, and this was apparent in his life. What did this mean about his relationship with God? Did he really know Jesus? Would he go to heaven? My brother in ministry told me once during my dad's illness that he had spoken with him about his relationship with God and that he believed he was a follower of Christ. I still had a twinge of concern, though, and needed assurance.

7

I also thought about his lack of forgiveness toward my mother for divorcing him, which had led to bitterness. He knew he was bitter because he and I had talked about it. Yet he could not bring himself to forgive and let go. He also had a strained relationship with another family member. Did he understand Christ's forgiveness toward him and our responsibility to forgive others?

I began to pray for two things: assurance that he would go to heaven, and assurance that he would find peace this side of heaven. What happens when someone has dementia? If he didn't know the Lord yet or if he knew Him but needed to reconcile his relationships, could God convict someone who was confused, had lost the ability to reason, and could not remember? But wait...it is not just reason that leads us to God! As a matter of fact, our own direction of reasoning can sometimes lead us away from Him if our focus on reasoning supersedes the quest for godly wisdom. Who would know that better than an analytical thinker? God's Word tells us that it is the *Holy Spirit* who convicts and reveals truth. What would this mean for my dad?

I recalled a trip I had taken with the youth from our former church a few years earlier. While there, we were to sing for residents of a nursing home in the dining area. Prior to singing, we went in small groups down the hallways visiting with residents in their rooms. The group I was with entered a room in which both ladies were confined to their beds. In talking with one of the ladies, it appeared that she likely had some form of dementia.

We asked the ladies if they would like us to sing for them since they would not be able to join us in the dining area. Both said they would like that. We began to sing "Amazing Grace," and the lady with what appeared to be dementia began to sing with us. She never missed a single word or note! I asked if I could pray with her before we left. She said she would like that also. I began to pray, and she began to pray, as well! She pleaded with her Lord to take her home...and how beautifully real and earnest her prayer was! She was so very connected to Him in spite of her confusion!

I was so overwhelmed with the realization that although the mind may be confused, the spirit is still connected to God! It does not matter what our state is here on this earth, our connection with our Creator is still there! He can still move our hearts, and He can still use us to bless others whether we realize it or not. She most likely had no idea, nor did her family members, how God had used her to bless me that day!

I have also seen this in working with individuals with developmental disabilities. I recall working with a lady for a while who was in a wheelchair. She would always say that when she got to heaven, she would be able to walk. I recently learned of her passing. I had a moment of sadness, but I was immediately reminded that she is now walking. I recall the huge smile that spread across her face when she would talk about someday walking in heaven. I was then overwhelmed with joy for her and the freedom of mobility she was now experiencing, as well as being in the presence of her Savior!

There is such a connection for some with God regardless of their intellectual limitations. Maybe there is a greater sense of the presence of a supreme God and other spiritual beings, as they may be more open to a level of spiritual awareness that makes so many others uncomfortable. I often think the rest of us are more limited or challenged in this area, as we tend to learn to become more self-reliant than dependent on God. We also become much more guarded in our thoughts, as well.

God's grace and power has no boundaries! He is the one and only sovereign God of the universe, *"the Most High...ruler over the realm of mankind"* (Dan. 4:17, 25, 32 NASB). Some translations use the term "kingdom" instead of "realm." We may try to establish our own kingdoms of sorts, based on what our culture considers relevant. But ultimately, God is sovereign over everything that takes place in our lives, our hearts, and our minds.

Maybe dementia can even be a blessing because it hinders our thought processes! I certainly have noticed a change in my cognitive function. Initially, I had an ongoing argument in my mind as to how an analytical thinker would be able to function if the thinker is not functioning as it previously has. My argument with myself was that I would need to depend on God more. Eventually, I believe that I accepted greater dependence on God as the answer as He has proven himself to be faithful so many times, even in the small things— such as forgetting where I have "safely" hidden things! I simply ask God to have mercy on this feeble mind and remind me where my "safe" places are!

So, the realization that God could work in my dad's mind and heart in spite of dementia gave me hope. I knew that regardless of what should happen over the next several years, God would still be able to reach my dad. Maybe God had allowed me to have that experience at the nursing home to prepare me for this season of my life. He never ceases to amaze me!

DIANE BENTLEY

# 2

# Role Reversal

In preparation for my dad's follow-up visit to the neurologist, my research had led me to a list of questions that should be asked of the physician when a diagnosis of dementia has been made. Those questions included whether it was still safe for him to drive and to live alone, among many others. I did not relish the thought of asking those questions in front of my dad. So, I contacted the doctor's office to try to arrange a discussion with his physician prior to the appointment. The office staff informed me that the doctor could only speak with me when my dad came in for an appointment. *Yikes!*

When we arrived for the appointment, I informed the staff members that I had some questions for the doctor. They took my dad back and then took me to a separate room to meet with his physician. I...being so prepared...pulled out my list of questions. I then asked the tough questions: How long would it be safe for my dad to drive? His physician's response was, "He should not be driving." *What?* I had been so prepared with my questions, but that was not the answer I was prepared to hear! Okay...next question: How long would it be safe for him to live alone? His physician's response was, "He should not be living alone." *What?* Once again, I was not prepared for that answer!

I proceeded to tell the doctor that my dad appeared to still have pretty good days during which he appeared to have very little cognitive impairment. The doctor told me that people who have this type of illness become very good at hiding things and covering them up, and he was basing his recommendations on my dad's EEG (electroencephalogram) results he had previously obtained, as well as his evaluations. I informed my dad's doctor that he would need to be the one to inform my dad that he should no longer drive, and that he would need to be the one to inform my dad that he should not be living alone. Wow...I anticipated this was going to be an interesting ride home! My thoughts were, *God, please help me... You are my protector, my shield! Can I* **please** *hide under the shelter of Your wings—***NOW***?* And I meant to *literally* **HIDE***!*

We entered the room where my dad and Kevin were. Kevin always went with us to my dad's doctor visits. Dad always took the days of medical appointments as opportunities to eat out, and Kevin was all about eating out! Actually, Kevin was all about eating—period. He began one meal already planning the next! Dad and Kevin also took this time to go shopping if they needed something and wanted me to assist them.

During this visit, however, the neurologist informed my father that he should not be driving, nor should he be living alone anymore. My father stated that he did not live alone, as Kevin was there with him. The neurologist cut his eyes toward me. What could I say? My dad never acknowledged during his illness that Kevin's presence in the home would not be sufficient for his care, other than at one point stating that Kevin was refusing to help him. My father then questioned why he should not be driving, and the neurologist attempted an explanation—which my father did not accept! He tried to explain the concerns with both dementia and parkinsonism, telling Dad that an individual who has just one of these illnesses eventually becomes unable to drive. The doctor then reiterated to my dad that he had both conditions, which made driving an even greater risk.

After we left the doctor's office, as we drove home my dad asked if I had told the doctor to tell him he could no longer drive. I thought, *Okay...here we go! Help me, Lord!* After a deep breath, I proceeded to explain to my dad that I had done research about his condition that recommended questions for his physician. After much discussion of the fact that all I had done was ask questions, Dad finally appeared to accept that this was not something I had caused. He then confessed that on a few occasions he had pulled up to a stop sign or a red light and did not know where he was. He also confessed that the road signs would change before his eyes. My heart sank as I became more acutely aware of my dad's condition. How many other things were happening that he was not revealing, things that had put him and Kevin at risk?

Over the course of the next year and few months, my dad's symptoms appeared to be stable. The medications appeared to be effective, though there were concerns regarding whether he was taking them accurately. Initially he refused assistance with them, but after two occasions of thinking he had not taken them but finding them missing, he relented. He insisted, however, that it be done his way (which I found to be more confusing, but I humored him), and that he be able to watch the medications being put into his dispenser. He hoped he would eventually be able to do this independently again, and he wanted to keep up with them by watching. He did eventually let it go and allowed me to fill the dispenser without his supervision. I took this opportunity to simplify the process!

He also continued to be hopeful that at some point the neurologist would allow him to drive again, as did Kevin. My dad asked at every appointment if he had improved enough to drive again. At least until he had declined to the extent that he was no longer concerned with driving. The neurologist never said "never," which was most likely best for everyone!

However, there were occasions in the beginning when my dad drove anyway! I am not sure he knew that we were aware. It was my aunt who initially realized what was happening. She would go over to his home when he was not there, and she realized that he was out driving. I am not sure if anything was said to him or not, but knowing how protective and concerned his sisters were, it likely was. He also continued to drive equipment such as a tractor. He did have a couple of mishaps at his home, and after that point, he appeared to be more willing to give up driving them.

One of those mishaps included the time when he drove his Explorer to hook up to a trailer in the yard. When he got out of the vehicle, he forgot to put it in PARK. The Explorer left without him! It rolled right through a chain-link fence, across a field, and to the edge of the woods. It stopped just short of a ravine from which it would have had to be pulled out had it gone in. Thankfully, no one was injured!

Family members had also observed Dad driving over a curb in a public parking lot. Dennis saw him park almost parallel in a non-parallel parking space. These two incidents occurred before the neurologist had told him he could no longer drive, and I had brushed them off as being related to his vision deficit. But now I was not certain these incidents were just vision-related.

My dad's siblings were very helpful by assisting him with meals. They also assisted him with getting Kevin to work on Saturdays. Kevin worked at a grocery store on Fridays and Saturdays for three hours each day. He had his transportation covered on Fridays by his day program provider. They had provided transportation on Saturdays in the past, as well, but they had changed their policy and no longer provided services on Saturdays. And so my dad had been taking him on Saturdays for a long time due to that change. This was one of Kevin and Dad's special times together. They always went out to breakfast prior to Kevin going to work. But at this point, Kevin needed other support for transportation.

Some of my dad's siblings also assisted with his medical appointments for quite some time. But I eventually began doing all of those, as well, to avoid confusion about medication changes, since I was responsible for preparing them for him to take. Assisting my dad with medical appointments was a full-time job in and of itself. I often jokingly stated he had a specialist for every system in the body. However, that was not far from the truth. When I think about it, I cannot think of many systems for which he did not see a specialist. Of course, that knowledge is not my area of expertise.

I continued to work during this time, as well. As long as his symptoms were stable, and we coordinated as many appointments as we could on the same days, I managed. But little did I know (although I should have), this was the calm before the storm!

It is often said that if you are not in the middle of a storm, you likely just came out of one or are headed into one. We often think of the storms of life negatively, and we wonder where God is and why He allows these struggles. I can personally testify that God has used these struggles to grow me and strengthen me in my faith, all the while transforming me into His likeness. I think of the struggles, including persecution, recorded in the Bible, and it is obvious to me that no one is immune to suffering. Not even the very Son of God lived on this earth without suffering. Oh, what suffering He endured, and all because of His love for you and me. He paid the ultimate price so that we would not be separated from our loving and merciful Father for eternity, and also so that we can have an abundant, victorious life while here on earth.

As a mother, it is so difficult to watch my children go through difficulties. I often think of Mary watching her son, the Son of God, being rejected, persecuted, beaten, and nailed to a cross. I cannot begin to imagine what that was like for her. I recall when God initially convicted me that it was time for me to let go and surrender my children. He reminded me that they were created by Him, for His purposes. I remember praying in total honesty that it just seemed a little cruel for moms to carry their children...to deliver them into this world... to nurture and care for them...to kiss their booboos...to battle the school system for them...and then to just have to let them go? In that moment, He reminded me that He, too, loved His Son so much, but He also had to let Jesus go, knowing what He would endure on this earth. But God allowed Him to come to the earth and endure great suffering because of His love for me and you!

And, I know, just as it is for me, that it is through the struggles my children endure that God will grow them. And seeing that growth brings such peace and joy! A parent's love can be heart-wrenching because we bring children into this world, and then we nurture, provide for, and protect them. Then they are suddenly grown, and there are things, events, or circumstances from which we cannot protect them. However, there is a heavenly Father who is continually with His children, and we can trust Him and know that *"all things work to-gether and are [fitting into a plan]for good to and for those who love God and are called according to [His] design and purpose"* (Rom. 8:28 AMP).

Now I was watching my dad go through a horrible illness that would bring him to tremendous dependence on others. It felt as though I was experiencing a role reversal with me becoming the parent and him becoming the child. That just did not feel right to either of us! Trying to balance allowing him as much independence as possible but ensuring his health and safety is no easy task—especially with someone who was as strongly independent as my dad. I was continuously reevaluating my dad's care and circumstances and questioning whether things should be done differently. Unfortunately, just as children do not come with a one-size-fits-all instruction manual, neither do aging parents with illnesses!

However, God knows our parents better than we know them—and better than they know themselves. He provides wisdom and understanding. Unfortunately, sometimes things are just learned the hard way... somewhat like our children (and us)! But I just needed to entrust my dad to God's care, as I had to do with my children, and trust in His guidance.

There is no script for this. No family is identical, and the battles before each family may vary somewhat. But the God of the universe sees and knows all. He knows our hearts and the hearts of our loved ones. We can trust Him with them. That trust in Him will get you through any fire, including caring for someone with dementia.

Yes, there was still much uncertainty, as so many questions remained unanswered. There are things that we experience in this life that we may never understand or receive answers for this side of heaven. However, I know that I know that I know, I can rest in God's embrace and trust in His promises. He is a loving and merciful God who so cares for us, in spite of our weaknesses and failures. He promises never to leave us nor forsake us, and that means to me that He is always there, providing everything I need. It might not be everything I want, but what I want might not always be what I need. He knows best, and we can trust in that.

And here in the midst of the uncertainty...in the storm surrounding us...there was a brief break in the clouds, a respite, so to speak. I thank You, Lord, for times of respite. He knows how much calm we need, exactly when we need it, and He is gracious to provide!

# 3

# Sufficiency of Grace

During this time of calm, I began the process of applying to graduate school, as I had felt the Lord leading me to get my master's degree in school counseling. I had argued that I should just apply for counseling rather than *school* counseling, although His leading had never been clearer and more specific to me than it was about this. I am not sure why I am still argumentative at times when it comes to God's direction. It never ends well for me, and He knows the future and the big picture when all I see is the here and now!

In any case, I had succumbed to the idea of school counseling, and I decided to apply, was accepted, and then was ready to start in March 2008. Just a week prior to starting classes, my father-in-law fell and chipped his hip bone. He had previously been diagnosed with lung cancer, among other health conditions. He left the hospital with hospice services, and my husband and his siblings alternated staying nights with him. My mother-in-law was providing all of his care during the day, and she needed support so she could rest at night.

In April 2008, my own dad fell and suffered a compression fracture to a vertebra. He was scheduled to see a physician's assistant with his primary care physician for follow-up to the emergency room visit. She had looked at his chart, saw that he was already seeing a physician due to his degenerated discs, and then contacted them. When we went in to the appointment, she informed us that she had already confirmed that they would perform a procedure called a kyphoplasty, and she had scheduled him to see the doctor there. However, from the time he fell until he had the procedure, he suffered in great pain.

For approximately two weeks, he was unable to do anything for himself and required constant assistance. My husband and I stayed with him during the week, and my brother and sister-in-law helped out on the weekend. His siblings were also in and out of the home.

During an unrelated visit to his urologist, my dad told his urologist that the pain medication for the fracture was not working, and that doctor prescribed something else for him, which included anti-nausea medication. My dad's dementia and Parkinson's symptoms were exacerbated by this medication. He was extremely disoriented, and his tremors were so violent that he would slide right out of the chair.

Fortunately—or not—since it was due to our having experienced it with my father-in-law's medication, we recognized the sudden changes as being medication related. He had had a similar reaction while on pain medication after chipping his hip bone. We immediately stopped this pain medication and went back to the initial pain medication that had been prescribed for my dad. I later was told by his neurologist that anti-nausea medications work through the nervous system and anyone with Parkinson's disease or dementia should not take them. Once the medication was out of his system, his symptoms improved tremendously.

My dad had the kyphoplasty for the compression fracture. He experienced immediate pain relief, and he was able to discontinue the stronger pain medications prescribed due to the fracture. I continued to assist with his medical appointments and medications.

In June 2008, both of my sister-in-laws were going on vacation during the same week, and there would be no family near my mother and father-in-law should they need someone to help. After discussion among the siblings, it was decided that they would stay with us during that week, and plans were made to move them in the weekend prior. If you have ever cared for someone who requires a lot of medical equipment, you can relate to what an undertaking that move was.

Then, on the day they were to move in, I woke up with a kidney stone. This was my first experience with kidney stones, but my sister informed me that this made me an official member of the family, since my dad, she, and another brother had all had them. I believe I would prefer another means to become an official member! I mean, seriously, is our biological connection not sufficient? I informed Dennis that I did not have time for a kidney stone, and he replied that I would have to make time (he had experienced kidney stones himself). As the pain intensified, I realized he was right. I went to the emergency room for pain management, then returned home and drank as much water and cranberry juice as I could tolerate, passed the kidney stone that night, and then moved the in-laws in the next day! No big deal, right?

I was also still taking classes during this time, as well as working and providing assistance to my dad. At the end of the week, when my sister-in-laws were to return home, we found out that one of them would be gone again in a couple of weeks. This sister-in-law was the one who had been most available to assist during the day due to her schedule. We convinced the in-laws to remain with us through that time so they would not have to pack up and leave and then move back again. My father-in-law loves cookouts. So, on the one occasion he talked about wanting to go home, I asked if he wanted to stay through July the Fourth and have a cookout. He did not ask to go home again—ever. Who knew a cookout was all that was needed to make him content with his current living arrangement!

We had the cookout, and most, if not all of Dennis's family members were present. His dad seemed to enjoy this so much, and we were able to take lots of pictures. I also was able to get signatures on a mat from family members to frame a picture from this cookout and give him for his upcoming birthday.

Over the course of these weeks with us, preceding the cookout we had noticed a significant decline in his condition. We were growing concerned about Dennis's mother being alone during the day with him, as well as his care becoming more than she could handle alone. Once again, after some discussion it was decided they should remain with us. It was not difficult to convince my mother-in-law, so I feel she sensed the need for more assistance, as well.

My father-in-law's birthday was July 29, and we began plans for another cookout for his birthday. Also, during this time my stepfather had fallen off a ladder and had surgery for hematomas on both sides of his brain. He had to go to rehab after the surgery, and my mother had to be with him, alternating days with his daughter. My mother was also providing care for my grandmother. When my mother had to be out of town with my stepfather, I assisted with my grandmother, which consisted of taking her a meal and supervising her evening medications. I joked at one point that I should just open a personal care home, as I would be able to completely fill it with our family members!

I share all this not to make myself appear as Wonder Woman or any other superhuman hero, which I can assure you I am not! I share this, rather, to reveal how so very sufficient God's grace is in the midst of difficult circumstances. And truthfully, *sufficient* seems such an inadequate word to describe God's grace. These were the kind of circumstances that, while in the midst of them, you just keep on keeping on, almost methodically. But you then look back and wonder how in the world you survived that! Caregiving can be difficult enough, but with all of this, I felt spread very thin over that summer. But I have learned that when walking through the fire, God always walks with you.

We had the cookout for my father-in-law's birthday the weekend prior to his birthday, which actually fell on a Tuesday. He was able to enjoy time with his family, and all of his children were able to be there. His birthday rolled around on Tuesday, and he was still alert and cognizant of the significance of the day.

On Wednesday, however, he began to deteriorate, and after speaking to a nurse with hospice, we realized that this was the beginning of his final journey to his eternal home. She informed us that often people will hang on for a special or significant day, and then begin the process of their physical departure. So, we felt he might have been hanging on to be able to celebrate his birthday. We were told we should begin contacting other family members to notify them of his condition, and we did so.

I obviously felt the need to be there with my family. We had people in and out for the next few days, and toward the last couple of days, people camped out everywhere in our home. I called it the "Invasion of the Bentleys," but without ill intent! However, I was still taking a class, so I emailed my professor to inform her of the circumstances, and she extended the deadlines for my assignments and assured me that she would be praying for the family.

My father-in-law went to his eternal home on August 2, and of course, there were a few more days of gatherings of family and friends. During all this time, I had very little time to work on my coursework, and the end of the term was approaching. I emailed my professor again to ask if an extension could be granted beyond the end of the term, knowing it would not be possible for me to complete all the work by that time. She responded that she could not, that all work would have to be completed by the end of the term.

I began working frantically to get it all done, which also included a lengthy research paper. The deadline for all work to be submitted was on a Sunday at midnight. While working on the Saturday just prior to the deadline, it became obvious that I would not be able to complete everything by Sunday. I began to pray, "Lord, I believe that You were leading me to go to school, and I know that I cannot complete all of this work by Sunday night. I need Your help." Within moments, maybe even seconds, a message came across the school website that the deadline for the end of the term had been extended to Monday at midnight, due to technical problems with the website. What? I personally had not had any problems with the website!

I took off work Monday and continued to push through, but I realized on Monday afternoon that I still would not be completely finished by midnight. I again appealed to God for grace. Yet *another* message came across the website stating that the deadline had been extended to Wednesday at midnight, due to continued technical problems with the website! I still had experienced no problems! I completed all my work and had it all submitted by Wednesday at 6 p.m.! Wow! God knew exactly how much time I needed, and He provided that with a few hours to spare! My thoughts were that I should call the school and let them know that if they would have granted me an extension, the website would likely have been fine. God is sovereign, and He was really in control of their website and the extensions!

What an awesome God we serve! How can I not trust Him at all times with everything? He is sovereign over all, and He provides for every need in every situation, including school deadlines! Psalm 135:5–6 states, *"For I know that the LORD is great and that our LORD is above all gods. Whatever the LORD pleases, He does, in heaven and in earth, in the seas and in all deeps"* (NASB).

God continued to provide faithfully, as in addition to caring for my dad, we also had my mother-in-law for approximately five weeks following her gall bladder surgery in 2009. She later fell...I believe in April 2010... and broke her hip. She was in and out of our home for eleven months after she broke her hip, between three surgeries and hospital visits, as well as rehab visits. She received therapy during this time in our home, as well.

I also continued working and assisting my dad and Kevin with medical appointments and medications, as well as grocery shopping. Again, my dad's medical appointments did not consist of primary care and a neurologist only. So, assisting him with medical appointments was much more involved than it would have been for other people. There were also surgeries at various times over the course of his illness. He had been diagnosed with bladder cancer years earlier, and he had a routine cystoscopy to ensure it had not returned. He also had cardiac-related procedures and surgery for aneurysms.

Due to all of the appointments and my job, I did withdraw from school in fall of 2009, as it became too overwhelming to keep up with the schoolwork in addition to everything else. My dad's condition fluctuated, which is most likely typical of this type illness. There are also other factors that can definitely contribute to variations in the severity of symptoms at different times.

Dad always appeared to be worse following surgical procedures. On one occasion while he was in the hospital, he wanted his shotgun because he was convinced there were bears in his room. On another occasion, I had waited until late in the evening to ensure he was okay before leaving the hospital. I spoke with the nurse and was assured that he would be fine if I went home. When I arrived the following morning, I was greeted by a nurse who appeared to be in a tizzy, as some might say. Upon seeing me, she immediately began to inform me that during a portion of the night, they had four nurses in my dad's room. He thought he had been kidnapped and wanted to get away!

Additionally, I could always see more severe tremors if he became upset about something. And as I mentioned before, different medications could impact his symptoms.

I was definitely beginning to see a progression in the illness, as well. And as I have said, I am a planner. So, I found a website that provided information about the stages of dementia and the symptoms that would be seen at each stage. I could definitely see my dad transitioning to a new stage in the progression of his illness.

On one occasion, I recall printing off the stages and symptoms. I highlighted the new symptoms I was seeing and took it to his neurologist during one of his appointments. He confirmed the progression of my dad's illness.

As things progressed, more decisions about care were needed. It is so very difficult to know what is best and then make those decisions. I tried to include my brother and sister in those decisions. But that was difficult, as well, since they did not see him as often as I did, and Dad could present himself in a better state when they were there visiting.

God's wisdom was and is the most important source for decision-making in any circumstance. Our perspective is not always aligned with God's. I have read through the Bible chronologically, which I highly recommend. One of the things that I was most struck by as a result is that during biblical times, people believed that everything that happens on earth is the result of activity in the spiritual realm. Even people of pagan religions in the Old Testament reportedly refer to actions of their gods in relation to what happened in their lives.

Our culture has led us away from this thinking, and we tend to compartmentalize God as being relevant only in certain areas of our lives, maybe also at specific times of our lives. But my God—the one, true God—is sovereign over all things. He created this world and human beings for His purposes. We are not here to see how much we can obtain, or how great a position we can achieve, though those things may happen in the process. But ultimately, we were created by God, for God...for His kingdom purposes!

God cares about even the seemingly smallest decisions we make. Each decision we make either leads us toward Him or away from Him. Some decisions are not that difficult, but others we stress and toil over. I have never been led astray when making decisions with God's provided wisdom and direction. Even when making decisions that revolved around my dad's care. I have been asked by younger mothers what my best advice would be. I do not have the answers for parenting, but I know the One who has all the answers. My best advice is to pray, pray, and pray. Ask for His wisdom in all things and seek his answers in His Word. He tells us that when we seek Him, we will find Him. So, seek Him, beloved child of the Lord Almighty. In the big *and* seemingly small things...seek Him.

DIANE BENTLEY

# 4

# Lessons Learned

Circumstances had settled down a bit. My stepdad had returned home, my father-in-law was now in heaven, and my dad was stable. My family decided to get away for a long weekend between my classes, which we did over the Labor Day weekend in 2008. We went horseback riding in the mountains, and I recall thinking, "I'm getting horse therapy"—and tears briefly trickled down my face. We explored a cavern while we were there, as well.

The beauty of the mountains was so relaxing. I have always felt the presence of God strongly when I am in the midst of His creation. We did not hike there during this trip, but to me the most relaxing part of God's nature is water, and I love, and am amazed by, the powerful force and sound of waterfalls. I also love hearing the magnificence of the ocean waves crashing onto the shore and the rushing roar of a flowing river.

Lakes are also relaxing, and I recall on one occasion walking to the lake near our home. This particular lake is very clear in comparison to others. On this occasion, I sat on the dock and could see a turtle walking around on the bottom of the lake. It is so amazing how God has provided all they need in their environment, and through that God reminded me that He would provide everything I needed to get through this season of life. I was reminded that was exactly what this was...a season of life. This struggle would not last forever. But I did not allow my thoughts to go there often, because I believed there was only one way this struggle could end.

While we were in the mountains, we saw many deer and turkey, and we spent some time at, and some of us in, the river. It was very therapeutic, considering the summer we had just experienced. It is extremely important as a caregiver to take time for yourself...to care for yourself. If you do not care for yourself, you will be less able to care for your loved ones. What that means for each of us is not likely the same. But be sure to know what you need to relax and have fun, and then make time for opportunities to do so. Dennis had told me on a few occasions that I had forgotten how to laugh. Take care to preserve your laugh and your joy.

I then had a couple of months following that were somewhat restful other than the routine care of medical appointments and medications for my dad. In November 2008 however, my dad had an eye surgery. As a result, the pressure in his eye was extremely high, and it was unable to be lowered to a safe level with eye drops alone. His physician ordered an oral medication to lower the pressure, which once again was a medication that exacerbated his dementia symptoms. He also experienced a lot of nausea due to the pressure in his eye, and he could not take anti-nausea medications, as I mentioned before. I found a ginger supplement that appeared to help with the nausea, but he was not doing well otherwise. His sister found him on the floor of his home one morning, and he was unable to get up. We were uncertain how long he had been there.

I spoke with the physician on call after this incident of finding him on the floor. After informing him of this and other incidents, I was told that if help was not provided in the home, he would likely soon be in a long-term care facility. I informed my siblings, and we all agreed to pursue hiring help for the home. I researched agencies and the cost and found one that seemed to be the best fit. We started out with help on a daily basis, including weekends and evenings.

Eventually, after several months, the pressure in my dad's eye was resolved, and he was able to come off the oral medication to lower the pressure. Once the medication was out of his system, we began to see improvements in the dementia, with the exception of his mood.

He became very agitated, and he was very unhappy having help in his home. He would shake his finger at me, and in very unsettling tones (I am trying to be nice here!), he would reprimand me for hiring the help. It was during this time that I began to question why I was the child there to provide the care. I was possibly the most sensitive sibling in the family, and I often had to leave my dad's home to get away from his derogatory remarks. I had to continuously remind myself that this was the illness talking, not my dad. Though the illness was responsible for his inability to reason, thus understanding his need for support in the home, I also believe it was responsible for removing those barriers that enable us to address issues with social graces intact!

My dad had also developed some obsessive-compulsive behaviors related to spending money. Paying for help was interfering with his spending, in addition to putting people in his home that he did not think he needed. I addressed the obsessive spending habits with his neurologist, who informed me that it was unusual for this to be part of the illness. However, after some research, my sister informed me that she'd read that obsessive-compulsive behaviors can be a side effect of the medication for the Parkinson's symptoms.

During this time, I was also receiving phone calls from Kevin stating he needed help. In his words, "help me out" could be the result of his frustration or it could sometimes be related to potentially serious issues. He usually described an incident that had occurred with Dad that had upset him. Sometimes he would tell on Dad for something he had said or done. On a couple of occasions, Kevin even reported physical aggression on both of their parts. Rest assured, outside the illness, this would never have happened. As I said before, my dad believed the world revolved around Kevin and what he wanted.

Kevin would also call out of concern about Dad wanting to ride equipment or do other things that Kevin recognized he should not be doing. During this time, Kevin appeared to begin to recognize some risks for Dad. Kevin appeared to be struggling emotionally, as well. He was beginning to recognize the decline we were all seeing, as well as living in what was probably a very stressful environment, although I am not sure Kevin actually understood what all of this meant.

Over the course of the spring and summer of 2009, my dad eventually "fired" most of his help. He started with the weekend help, and we were in agreement with this decision because he was doing better, and we had family members who would check on him over the weekend to make sure he was okay. But then Dad began to request that no one come in the evenings. His siblings were helping with meals and were in and out in the evenings, and I could be there some evenings, too, so we discontinued the evening staff, as well. Toward the end of 2009, my dad moved my brother in the home with him. He insisted that if this worked out well, he would no longer need paid staff during the day, either. Within a few months, Dad took it upon himself to discontinue the paid help on weekdays, too, though he really needed their support. Due to both of my brothers's impairments, my dad's needs required a greater level of care than they could handle responsibly.

I had also experienced some changes in my job during the same month my dad had his eye surgery in 2008, which added tremendously to my workload. I was struggling to meet my deadlines, and with this added pressure in addition to the stress of my dad's needs, I had allowed it to make me feel badly about myself.

By the fall of 2009, I was struggling as—and I am going to use the horrible M word here—menopause had hit, as well, and in full force, I might add! It is possible that the stress of my job and the situation with my dad had exacerbated the menopause symptoms, but for whatever reason...I was going CRAZY due to a lack of sleep! I could barely handle being around myself, so I can only imagine what it was like for those around me! The enemy of my soul was having a field day with my mind...with my permission! I was believing his accusa-tions, allowing him to rob me of my peace and the joy of my salvation.

In September 2009, I went to my doctor and de-scribed my symptoms to her. I always prefer to try nat-ural solutions first, and she gave me a list of things for which she had read research that had been documented to be effective. I went to the local health store and asked for one of the items. The very kind lady in the store re-sponded that this particular item worked very well—and she knew because she had been using it for fifteen years! WHAT? Now, I am typically a quiet, gentle spirit, but you have to know, I had only been getting three to four hours of sleep per night for several weeks. I yelled (I have been told that my yelling is not really "yelling," because I am so soft-spoken), "FIFTEEN YEARS?! HOW LONG DOES THIS TAKE?" The kind lady just looked at me, and her expression said, *Oops...I should not have said that!* Just so you know, I did apologize to her the very next time I was in her store to purchase my supply—which did work! Dennis and I both were very thankful that it worked! She was very gracious, and she denied even remembering the incident.

It was during this time that I had to withdraw from school. However, I believe God had already accom-plished what He was doing through the school counseling program. I took a course in Foundations of Education, which turned out to be one of the most inspiring and thought-provoking classes I had ever taken. It gave me a burden that people are not prepared for what lies ahead. I cannot tell you what lies ahead, but I am concerned—no, convinced—that people, including some in the church, are not prepared. This burden has become even more intense in recent weeks.

The class from which I had to withdraw, Cultural Diversity, also made me more acutely aware of how influenced we are by our culture to the extent of indoctrination of ideas or values that are inconsistent with God's truth. We become so assimilated within our culture that our thoughts on various issues seem so "normal" to us that we don't question the validity of it in light of God's truth.

This class also required me to examine my own cultural background, which can be very enlightening. It opened my eyes to family issues that I had also struggled with over the years. The timing...God's timing... was perfect, as I was struggling with some questions. Is His timing not always perfect in spite of the timing we desire?

As I stated previously, I was struggling with why I was the sibling among my brothers and sister who was providing all of Dad's care at this time. After a few weeks or months of questioning why, I decided to make my nights of sleeplessness (though this had improved) a time of prayer. I quit asking why and asked the Lord to teach me what He wanted me to learn through this experience. What a loaded request this can sometimes be, and I find that He is so very happy to oblige! There were many lessons and revelations He provided related to my childhood during this time, which gave me a greater understanding of my dad.

When I made a conscious decision to allow God to teach me, He gave me a verse to a song. When I was much younger—a little less than thirty years prior—God had begun to give me songs. Prior to that, I had been writing poetry, but I had never written a song. However, when my parents divorced, I quit writing anything, as well as quit playing music and singing. I went through a period of time that I refer to as "my time of wandering in the wilderness." When God led me out of the wilderness and drew me back to Him, I did begin to write poetry again, but this was the first time a song had been given to me since my parents' divorce. However, only the first verse had come to me by the end of 2009.

I continued to pray for God to teach me through these difficult circumstances, and then one Sunday my pastor spoke on the topic of anxiety. I also listened to a message online by a pastor I knew, which turned out to be a similar message. Obviously, God was trying to show me something here. So, when I asked, He revealed to me that I had caused great anxiety in my life because I had made myself so overly responsible for my father. I felt responsible to the extent that I believed that if something happened to him, it would be because of something I did or did not do...as if I have that kind of authority over someone else's life! I surrendered my dad's well-being to God's care, and what a relief! I felt as though several tons of weight had been lifted from my shoulders.

God laid a passage of scripture, Psalm 63, on my heart.

*O God, You are my God; I shall seek You earnestly; my soul thirsts for You, my flesh yearns for You, in a dry and weary land where there is no water. Thus I have seen You in the sanctuary, To see Your power and Your glory. Because Your lovingkindness is better than life, My lips will praise You. So I will bless You as long as I live; I will lift up my hands in Your name. My soul is satisfied as with marrow and fatness, and my mouth offers praises with joyful lips. When I remember You on my bed, I meditate on You in the night watches, For You have been my help, and in the shadow of Your wings I sing for joy. My soul clings to You; Your right hand upholds me. But those who seek my life to destroy it, Will go into the depths of the earth. They will be delivered over to the power of the sword; They will be a prey for foxes. But the king will rejoice in God; Everyone who swears by Him will glory, For the mouths of those who speak lies will be stopped* (NASB).

Do you see what this passage says about the enemy who wants to destroy our lives? Yet, we are upheld by God's own right hand! God is worthy of our praise regardless of our circumstances or how we feel! It is through our praise and the sword of the Spirit, in spite of our struggles, whether illness, finances, or broken hearts, that we have victory over the enemy! The victory has already been won, but we so often fail to acknowledge it and realize it in our lives.

After reading this passage of Scripture, the remainder of the song God had begun to write in my heart came to me, and the song in its entirety is below.

## Verse 1
*Lord, now I come to You.*
*Just as I am, I come to You.*
*In need of Your love, mercy, and grace.*
*Lord, I bow before Your throne.*
*Just as I am before Your throne.*
*Take me to Your place of peace and rest.*

## Chorus
*You are my strength when I am weak.*
*I rest beneath the shelter of Your wings.*
*You are my help in time of need,*
*And I will praise You, Lord.*

## Verse 2
*Now I lay me at Your feet,*
*emptied of pride and self-defeat.*
*Fill me with Your fullness, O Lord.*
*I surrender all my thoughts and plans.*
*I know my life is held within Your hands.*
*I will cling to You, the great I Am.*

Whether providing care during illness or dealing with any other difficult circumstance, I learned to rest in the arms of God. I truly could trust that He was my help and my shelter. He is my strength, and there is peace and rest in Him, regardless of our circumstances.

Circumstances such as these result in a roller coaster of emotions. I learned to repeat to myself, "Emotions are real and must be dealt with, but emotions are not dependable, and they cannot always be trusted." I continuously repeated those words to myself to prevent the hostile takeover of those emotions. I learned to test my emotions to ensure they did not lead to irrational thoughts. That does not mean that I never had any. Obviously, I did, in thinking that I was fully responsible for the outcome of the care of my father. However, when they appeared to be creeping up, I turned to the truth of God's Word to take them captive.

During the times when my dad seemed to regress to his past, failing to recognize the present, he seemed to be lost in time. However, there were moments when I felt lost in time, as well. I felt as though the world was moving forward around me, but I was at a standstill. I recall wondering how God could use me during this time. Don't get me wrong—I fully believe that I was honoring God in caring for my dad. Maybe I just wanted to do more, but I felt as though I could not.

One night while I was praying, I asked God how He could use me. The following morning, I was awakened to the vision of a friend crying. This was not like a dream, during which there is activity. This was just a vision of her crying. I sensed that I needed to pray for her, and later in the morning I tried to call. I left a message letting her know that I had prayed for her as I had been led by God's Holy Spirit. I received a message from her later in the day, letting me know she got the message, that there had been an issue, and that I could be assured that God had been leading me to pray for her.

Yes, God had led me to pray specific prayers for specific individuals in the past, but this time I needed the urging of the Holy Spirit to pray as much as the recipient needed the prayer! God answered MY prayer by leading me to pray FOR SOMEONE in need of prayer! I might not have been able to physically be somewhere else during this time, but I could pray for others! And with the leading of the Holy Spirit, I can pray for the specific needs of others! Caregiving can be EXTREMELY overwhelming. But yes, there are other ways God can use you during this time, as well. I believe He also uses caregivers or others who are in the midst of a struggle by enabling us to get through it with an ounce of cognition and sanity remaining. Although this could be debated about myself! When others can see the peace and joy of God in spite of our circumstances, what a testimony that is.

God taught me another invaluable lesson during this time. I had struggled greatly with insecurity as a teenager. God had brought those memories and feelings to the surface when I began assisting my dad, and actually, even prior to that time when he lost a brother. During a much-needed vacation in the midst of my dad's illness, I was walking along the beach when I spotted a sand dollar. I picked it up for examination, and it was as close to perfect as any sand dollar I had ever observed. There were no chips or cracks, and the coloring was perfectly even. I held on to it and continued my walk.

Farther along the beach, I observed another sand dollar and picked it up. This sand dollar was not chipped or broken, either. However, after picking it up, I realized it had some discoloration covering approximately one-third of the sand dollar. I stooped to put the sand dollar down and was immediately stopped, in this very awkward position, as God's sweet voice whispered words of encouragement to me. Though the second sand dollar was discolored, it was just as important and valuable in God's eyes as the first.

There is no such thing as perfection in frail humanity. And as God had shown me many years ago, He reminded me now in the midst of this storm that it is His mercy, His righteousness in me, that matters, and nothing else. He meets us exactly where we are, but He has no intention of leaving us there! In our relationship with Him, He is continuously transforming our likeness to His. Though I will not get completely there while here in this earthly life, He continues His work in my life: *"For I am confident of this very thing, that He who began a good work in you will perfect it until the day of Christ Jesus"* (Phil. 1:6 NASB).

I questioned myself so much. Did I do enough for my dad? Did I do too much? Did I do things the way they needed to be done? Did I make the right decisions? There is so much involved in caregiving and so many factors to consider. Family dynamics are very different, as are the lives and seasons of life of the caregiver as well as the one who is receiving care. There is no perfection in this, either. You do the best you can with what you have...and at times I felt I had little to offer because I felt I was stretched so thinly.

However, my God, who is all-knowing, was with me, carrying me all the way. During the difficult times, I am certain there was only one set of footprints. Actually, I am certain that the majority of the time, there was only one set of footprints.

Life has a way of throwing things at us, and at times it seems so many difficulties crash in all at once. Hence the scripture, *"we are afflicted in every way, but not crushed; perplexed, but not despairing; persecuted, but not forsaken;*

struck down, but not destroyed" (2 Cor. 4: 8–9 NASB). What encouragement! And the verses preceding and following these two verses give the explanation as to why these trials do not have to crush us. It is absolutely the only way I know to survive the difficulties of this life. In 2 Corinthians 4:7, 10, Paul states, *"But we have this treasure in earthen vessels, so that the surpassing greatness of the power will be of God and not from ourselves;...always carrying about in the body the dying of Jesus, so that the life of Jesus also may be manifested in our body"* (NASB). What an amazing treasure, indeed!

God provided an additional reiteration of a known truth during these years, as well. For whatever reason— stress, menopause, or a combination of the two—I was experiencing what I considered to be significant hair loss. At one point, I was able to see a difference around my facial hairline. Fortunately, I initially had very thick hair, and I was told by my stylist that my hair volume was just becoming more typical, and actually still thicker compared to others!

One day I was cleaning the bathroom, including sweeping up all the hair. I remarked that it must be a full-time job for God to keep up with the number of hairs on my head! In that moment, He reminded me that He knows exactly the number of hairs on my head at any given time of any given day. He knows all the details of my life, including my physical, emotional, and spiritual needs and struggles. He knows because He cares and loves me so much that He is aware of everything! There is such comfort in knowing that the Creator of the universe, the one true God, the great I Am, cares to know all about me!

What peace and comfort that brings in times of trouble! God is all-knowing and all-powerful. He is the only source of enduring peace and joy regardless of our circumstances. He is the only reason that we can avoid total devastation in the midst of life's suffering! Regardless of the storm you are in or have been in, God can speak perfect peace to your being when your mind rests on Him. Let Him!

# 5

# Laughter is Great Medicine

Over the course of the remaining years, it became detrimental to my well-being to maintain my sense of humor. I want to dedicate this chapter to now-humorous events. I refer to them as "now-humorous" because at the time they occurred, some events were not so humorous—at least not to me!

By compiling them into one chapter, you may feel free to mark it and return to it when you need a laugh or two. You probably do not want to hear all the gory details, but I have to share a few stories, just because it is so important for caregivers to be able to laugh. I do not mind it being at our expense if it helps you! Just don't tell Dennis!

Dennis and I joked then, and we still do periodically, that there is a certain restaurant (which shall remain unnamed) that has a MOST WANTED poster on the wall of their men's restroom with my dad's and Dennis's pictures on it. On one occasion, while we were dining in this restaurant, my dad got up to go to the restroom, and he stopped suddenly and stated he did not make it! Dennis assisted him with getting to the bathroom, and once there, he became acutely aware of the extent of this accident. He suggested my dad let him throw his underwear in the trash. My dad's response was, "Do you want to throw my pants in the trash, too?" Dennis informed him that he might get arrested if he left the restroom with no pants at all, and so Dad agreed to keep his pants on! Thank You, Lord, for not-so-small favors!

Although I am so relieved that Dennis was handling that situation, it could have been interesting to have been able to observe, or at least hear, the conversation between them! They were in there so long during this time that the waiter came to the table and asked me if I wanted him to check on them. I think that would have been even worse for Dennis! What a trooper he was during all this! I could not have done any of it without his help and support! He is amazing!

On that same day, my dad had another appointment that we needed to go to after we ate. Dennis suggested, by phone...from the bathroom, that we might want to cancel his next appointment due to the accident. After seeing the front of my dad's pants when they came out, I disagreed and stated we should go ahead with it while we were there. After all, he only had one small wet spot on the front of his pants. However, once we were at the doctor's office, and my dad got out of the car, I saw the back of his pants... "Whoa!" Dennis asked if I had misunderstood and thought the accident was urine! The answer was a resounding "YES!"

My dad's procedure that morning was a cystoscopy to check for the reoccurrence of bladder tumors. This procedure sometimes made urination more urgent, so naturally I had assumed that was the issue. During our phone conversations from the bathroom, Dennis had never specified what type of accident had occurred! I then suggested we cancel the appointment, and Dennis refused. He said we were already there, and we were going to get it done! Well...okay, then!

On another occasion, after my dad had lost a significant amount of weight, my brother and I were transferring him from his wheelchair to his car. Once he stood up, his pants fell to the ground! In the parking lot! Of the same restaurant! He did not keep his pants on this time, but it was not intentional! I scanned the parking lot quickly for law enforcement (actually for ANYONE!) and was relieved to find no one around. An arrest for indecent exposure would not be the way my dad would want to be remembered in his final days, I am sure!

In addition to his obsessive spending habits, my dad would periodically develop obsessions over other things. For a period of time, his obsession was ink pens. Don't ask me why, because I have no logical explanation. It just was what it was! Every time I took him to the doctor, he would ask if the pens on the desk were for taking. He would usually add, "That looks like a good pen." Everyone was gracious and allowed him to take a pen.

On one occasion, he was at the nurses' desk rather than at the receptionist's desk and he saw a container of pens. He asked if they were available to take, and they accommodated him as usual. He reached into the pen holder with multiple pens and pulled out a silk flower. He put it in his pocket as he typically did with all the pens he had been collecting. I was not certain if he realized he had taken a flower with no pen attached, as some offices had attached a flower to each pen. But he never asked for a pen again. I so would have loved to know what his thoughts were regarding that event!

Then there were the behaviors! Oh my... I sometimes felt the need to hang a sign around his neck stating, "Excuse my behavior, I have dementia"! Of course, I did not do that, although it was very tempting. Sometimes Dad would make a derogatory statement toward someone, or he would just give a stare or an attempt to quietly share his opinion with those who were with him. However, he had a hearing deficit, and so what seemed like "quietly sharing" to him, I can assure you was not quiet enough for me!

And then there was Kevin. Dear, sweet Kevin, who just says what is on his mind regardless! Sometimes that is great, and at other times, not so much! During the time when my dad was on the medication that exacerbated his symptoms, I was at the home with him and Kevin. My dad was very disoriented and delusional. He would go through the motions of eating, but he had nothing in front of him. He would also point into the air as though something was there. But if there was something there, we could not see it! He would talk about needing to get his boots on and get on his tractor. He would also talk about work as though he was working at the job from which he had retired.

On one occasion, Kevin and I were sitting with my dad while he was going through the motions of eating and pointing up in the air. Kevin would look at me, then point to my dad, and I would just nod my head. He did this a couple of times, and I had thought, "I wonder what Kevin might be thinking." Almost immediately after that thought entered my mind, Kevin said, "He's crazy!" I no longer had to wonder what Kevin was thinking! I did try to explain to Kevin that this was happening due to the medications, but I am not sure if he got it. There was a lot he probably did not understand, and that might have been a good thing.

Another story that includes Kevin makes me laugh now. I was not laughing so much at the time! It is one of those episodes I refer to as "now-humorous"! I was doing the grocery shopping for Kevin and my dad. My dad continued to insist that he needed to go with us, though his mobility had deteriorated tremendously. Kevin was typically better able to tell me what they needed than my dad anyway, but he still insisted he should go, as well. However, he had begun to use the motorized carts, as he could not stand long enough to get through the store.

On this particular occasion, he seemed more confused than he typically was in the store. He was following Kevin and me in his cart. However, at the end of an aisle, we went left, but for some unknown reason he went right. Kevin called out, "No, Daddy, this way!" My dad immediately turned his cart to the left, whipping around—right into a display full of packets of...something! The display fell, and multitudes of these small packets fell to the floor. I straightened the display and knelt to pick up the packets as Kevin stood and watched. I looked up at him and asked if he could not help. You will need to add very strong sarcasm to my voice to get an accurate picture of this scene!

Kevin knelt down to assist me, and we finally got all the packets picked up and placed on the display. As we started down the next aisle, Kevin started mumbling, "Bad driver, bad driver"! I am laughing as I type this, but I was not laughing at all that day! I responded by asking Kevin if he now understood why Daddy could not drive a car. He nodded and never asked if the doctor would let Daddy start driving again. See, until this happened, Kevin had still held out hope and wanted to find out at every doctor's appointment if our dad had improved enough to start driving again, as did Dad himself. Again, it was one of those things Kevin did not get—at least not until this incident.

Now, let's get back to our shopping trip. Yes...there is more! As my dad followed us down the next aisle, he bumped into another display! However, I saw him before he completely knocked it over, and it was just tilted and ready to fall at any second! I called out to him to stop the cart and not move. I got to the display and held it up while he backed away. For the remainder of the trip, up and down the aisles, Kevin and I agreed that Kevin would block for my dad. Whenever there was a display, Kevin would stand between my dad and the display! We made it through the remainder of the shopping trip without further incident, and we did finally make it home! Again, thank You, Lord, for not-so-small favors!

My goal in this chapter is to provide a little humor to lighten things up during difficult times. So, I want to share a couple of Kevin stories that relate to some extent to my dad. Kevin goes to a day program, and he was arriving home from his program at the same time my dad was arriving with the aide assisting him at the time. My dad's mobility was already limited, and he was slow getting in and out of the car. As a result, Kevin was usually the first one in the house.

One day, Kevin went into the house, and then he immediately walked back out and calmly stated to everyone that there was a snake in the house. Well, he was so calm that no one believed him. However, my dad has always had a very strong respect for the potential risks of being in close proximity to...okay, he has a FEAR of snakes. Yes, there it is! I have put his fear out there. I have been told that this fear was the result of my dad being chased by a snake as a child. Reportedly, his siblings did not believe his story and laughed at him. Regardless of the reason for his fear, he refused to get out of the car until someone made sure there was no snake in the house. My dad's aide calmly went inside. But from what I understand, she immediately came back out screaming, "SNAKE, SNAKE," and flailing her arms! For the best laugh, I wish you could see Kevin describe her quick exit from the house. Now the only person left to save the day was the case manager who had taken Kevin home. He went inside and got the snake out using a tool he just happened to have with him.

My dad loved gardening and yard work (as long as there were no snakes around)! That was his heart and soul, and he would spend hours upon hours growing a garden large enough to feed an army when we were growing up. That is possibly an exaggeration by me, as I had to work in it while I was growing up! On one occasion, I decided the okra stalks were so tall and thick that I was sure I would not be able to find my way home without cutting some down! Since then, Dad had downsized, but he still liked having a garden, and with some help, he had continued this hobby. He had been having problems with deer getting into the garden, so he put a radio out in the garden to keep them out. However, Kevin had a different perspective. His case manager asked him if the radio was to keep the deer out of the garden. Kevin responded that the radio was not to keep the deer out, but it was there so the deer could dance! Sometimes I think I like his view of things best—just sometimes.

I have sometimes thought that once in heaven I will be more like Kevin. I believe that persons with Down syndrome have been given the gift of eternal innocence. Though circumstances and others can sometimes try to take that away, Kevin continues to have unconditional love. His love is for people. There is no pursuit of knowledge or position. Although Kevin does think he wants to achieve a higher position until an explanation of the amount of work required is given, he just loves people. It often seems life is just a big celebration to him. I believe that in heaven I will be in continuous celebration and worship of a Father and Savior whose unconditional love provided for me to be there! As I stated previously, Kevin is continuously planning parties and is very good at delegating assignments to others to make his parties happen. Therefore, we have our own personal party planner.

As my dad's illness progressed and he was having difficulty swallowing, he had a swallow study done. I was told that he would need to be prompted to swallow and if he continued to hold food in his mouth he would likely aspirate. On one occasion, after he began to live with me, I was assisting him with his meal. He was holding the food in his mouth, and I believe he had been aspirating, so I began to prompt him. I was pretty persistent because he had lost so much weight, and I wanted to get all the nutrition I could into him. He finally responded, "Swallow, swallow, swallow, swallow." Now, in order to get an accurate picture of the message he was conveying, I need you to add a lot of sarcasm to those words and repeat them quickly! I looked at him, and realizing how frustrating this must be for him, I gave him my blessing to go ahead to spit it out!

Also, during the time that my dad was living with us, he asked the hired caregiver if *I* had moved in with *him*. He did not realize he was not at his own home, and I did not plan to cause any unnecessary agitation or other negative feelings by clarifying. He also asked if Dennis had started working there. I am not sure where he thought he was at that time. We just went along with him, as did our wonderful help! She so understood the needs of someone with this illness, and she was truly a blessing from God.

About a year prior to my dad's diagnosis, Austin was a senior in high school. He played football and had a preseason game out of town. My dad and Kevin rode with us to the game, as did Joshua, who had graduated previously that year. During one of the plays, one of the players did not get up. We were looking for Austin on the field to make sure it was not him. Unable to find his number, we finally realized that it was him on the ground. He was not moving. We sat, waiting for him to get up. That is usually what happens...the trainer comes out and assesses the injury, and then the player gets up and walks off the field with assistance.

However, Austin was not getting up. The announcer came over the loudspeaker requesting that Austin's father come to the field. Joshua stood up in front of me and kept repeating, "Moms don't go on the field," as though I did not know that already! I just looked at him and sat there, anxiously awaiting good news. But then I saw an ambulance pull up. I looked at Joshua and said, "Now moms DO go on the field," and I left the stands and made my way to the football field.

I was nearing the huddle around Austin when I heard something behind me. I turned and looked, and my dad and Kevin both had followed me onto the field! It was the whole clan! On the football field! It was such a good thing that Austin could not see us for the huddle! Would he have been embarrassed? I will let you answer that for yourselves.

I rode in the ambulance to the hospital with Austin. He had dislocated his shoulder, which had made it difficult for him to move and get up. It was also uncertain on the field what the extent of the injury was, so moving him might have risked further injury. He did recover with no complications.

I previously mentioned that I had also assisted my mother with my grandmother's care during my dad's illness, as well. She had a heart attack and a stroke shortly after her ninety-fifth birthday, and she continued to have small strokes after that. She eventually developed a form of dementia, possibly what is called stroke-related dementia. My grandmother was a petite lady, only four feet and nine inches in height.

When we were visiting my grandmother on one occasion, my boys were measuring themselves against her height and excited that they were taller. They were at that age when surpassing the height of other family members gave them great joy and pride. As a matter of fact, they had made it such a competition with my dad that when he lost an inch after his compression fracture to a vertebra, he asked me not to tell Joshua and Austin that he was shorter! Sorry, Dad, your secret is now out!

My grandmother was trying to explain to my family that she had shrunk in height over the years according to measurements from the doctor's office. She told us that she used to be ten feet and four inches tall, but she was now four feet and nine inches! Whoa...that is some serious shrinking! Obviously, she meant to say four feet, ten inches!

On one occasion, I was sitting with my grandmother, and it was time to assist her with getting in bed.

My grandmother loves animals...and she always has. She took care of the neighborhood animals...or at least those in our family. It seemed to me at one point that the animals knew they should go to her if they were sick or injured...but maybe that's just my child's view! My mother had cats...plural...meaning she had downsized to just three cats! I am not a huge fan of cats, but I do love dogs! I apologize to the cat lovers reading this, but I cannot help how I feel! I thought animals were really smart, and they could sense if someone did not want to be around them. That was not the case with my mother's cats! I seemed then, and still do, to be a magnet to them!

Anyway, I was assisting my grandmother with getting into the bed, but one of the cats kept jumping onto the bed. It always landed in the spot where she would be lying down, so I would pick it up and set it on the floor. After several repetitions of this process, my grandmother told me to "leave the cat alone"! On another occasion, I was sitting across from her in the family room at my mother's house, and one of the cats continuously jumped up in my lap. I kept putting the cat down in the floor, but it would jump up again. My grandmother leaned forward in her chair and said, "You are not a very nice girl!" Just don't mess with the animals around my grandmother!

On one occasion after moving my brother (who had the impairment) in with him, I was taking my dad to the doctor. He had begun to want my brother to go back with him, stating that my brother knew and could report everything that needed to be reported to the doctor. This is the brother with the impairment whose perception of what needs to be reported and the accuracy of it would likely not be helpful to medical professionals. So, we were at an appointment...the four of us...my dad, Kevin, my brother, and me. My dad insisted that my brother should go back with him, and they both had been insisting all day that he had to be fasting for this appointment. I tried to tell them...all day...that he did not have to be fasting for this appointment because this office never did labs.

When we went back, my dad and brother mentioned to the nurse that he had fasted for the labs. She informed them that there would be no lab work and that he did not have to be fasting. She looked at me as though asking with her eyes if all were okay. The room was very small, and she suggested that we might not all be able to be in there. I suggested my brother go back to the waiting area, as I needed to be there, and he agreed. When he left, the nurse asked me if I lived with them. I responded that I did not live with them and I could go home. And I quite possibly sounded a little too happy about that (which I considered a wonderfully good thing). With concern in her voice and facial expression, she asked who took care of them, referring to my dad, Kevin, and my brother. I looked at her and smiled and replied, "They take care of each other...welcome to my world!" Though she seemed concerned, she did not pursue the matter any further.

Some events can seem both humorous and sad when relating to illness such as dementia. Sometimes I can look back and smile and laugh at things that at the time did not seem humorous. I can also see the sadness in those events, as well. However, it is so important to be able to make light of some situations and maintain your sense of humor. Dennis is so much better at making things feel more lighthearted in what may be an intense situation than I am. I appreciate his efforts to do that for me.

Having worked in the human service field most of my life, as well as providing care for so many family members, I can be too serious and intense at times. Allow yourself to laugh during difficulties, especially when providing care. Let the joy of the Lord be your strength. He truly can provide both peace and joy in spite of the circumstances you are facing. It is something that I find difficult to explain. It just has to be experienced. I pray that is your life's experience.

# 6

# Loss in Bits and Pieces

Watching my dad decline was a very sad and difficult thing. There were times when I felt too emotionally drained to provide what my dad needed. Dennis is
so very good at keeping things lighthearted when you
need them to be, as is one of my children.

My oldest son, Joshua, recently read a story about a
family member of someone with dementia in addition
to his own firsthand personal experience. He had these
thoughts to share: "If I ever have Alzheimer's, please put
a sign on my door that reads, 'If I am having a good day
today and know who you are, please love on me, pray
with me, and reminisce about the good times. If I am
having a not-so-good day and don't know you, PLEASE,
PLEASE, PLEASE have some fun at my expense! But
above all else, there is to be absolutely no crying. If you
do, I will think you are crazy because I have no clue who
you are and why you are crying in my room!'"

I love this, but the loving on and praying and reminiscing with is much easier than the not crying. Sorry, Sunshine...but I describe having a loved one with dementia as being in a constant state of grieving because you are losing bits and pieces of the person all along the way prior to the physical loss. That does not mean that you are constantly crying or sad. It just means there is a continuous sense of loss, which at times can be overwhelming.

My dad was the go-to guy to find out how to get somewhere. He could tell you how to get anywhere from anywhere. I recall the first time I realized he had lost that. He wanted to make a stop on the way home from a medical appointment, but he was unable to tell me how to get there. Fortunately, I was able to decipher just enough information he was providing to figure it out myself. This might not appear to be a major loss to others. But it was tremendous to me! It was such a huge part of who he was.

On one occasion, my dad had decided to take Kevin to a NASCAR race for his birthday. Kevin loved NASCAR, and his favorite driver was Kasey Kahne at the time, but he has since retired . My brother and his family were living in North Carolina at the time, and they met us for the Charlotte race. It was the perfect race for

Kevin because our seats were right in front of Kahne's pit and...Kahne won the race!

Following the race, everyone was in a rush to get out, and the rest of the family was far ahead of me and Dennis. I looked back and saw my dad. It was the first time during his illness that I recall seeing a look of panic on his face. He was frantically looking around, but he could not find any of us and he was just standing in place. I called out to Dennis, who stopped, and I went back to my dad. I took my dad's hand, and he said, "I can do this." I did not say anything but quietly held on to his hand with one and held on to Dennis with the other (for my sake)! Once we were away from the crowd and saw the remainder of the family, I let go of my dad's hand so he would not have to have them witness him being led out.

I also recall an occasion when I had a great idea... at least I thought...to take my dad to the mountains to see the Christmas lights. He absolutely loved Christmas lights, and I wanted him to experience the volume of lights I had seen when I had been there a few years prior. So, we planned a trip, and my sister decided to go with us. She is a teacher and was out of school for the holidays, so we planned the trip for shortly after Christmas. I wanted to do this before his condition worsened...or so I thought.

We all loaded up and went. But my dad was miserable. He could no longer tolerate the cold. We knew we would need a wheelchair for the location where we were going to see the most lights, and we kept him wrapped up well in the chair...at least we thought. We were there only a few days. The morning after we returned home, my dad had to be taken to the emergency room because he had developed pneumonia. He always said the trip made him sick. It was a trip well intended to do something for my dad that I knew he loved. But maybe I had waited too late in the progression of the illness?

Dad was also really good with numbers...math. Yet at some point he could not even balance his checkbook or manage his money. He was also a strong, determined man who eventually could not get himself to the bathroom.

I recall times when while with him, I had to fight really hard not to cry. I did try hard, Sunshine! When I was unsuccessful, I just had to walk away and give myself a time-out! Not the disciplinarian type of time-out—just a moment to breathe and remember that God is still sovereign and is still holding on to me. I recently thought in depth about the scripture Isaiah 49:16: *"See, I have engraved you on the palms of my hands..."* (NIV). Do you know how tightly you have to hold on to something in order to engrave it on the palm of your hand? That is how tightly God is holding on to you! Remember that during times of struggle, sadness, joy...whatever the season of life! The enemy wants to destroy you, but God is holding on so tightly to His children! Oh...if we would just find rest and peace in that and not become complacent or lose our way!

Yes...even in seasons of joy, the enemy can gain a foothold if we become complacent. Unfortunately for us, it does not take a large opening for the enemy, who wants more than anything to destroy us! But thankfully, there is a way out! Even when we sometimes lose our way temporarily, there is a way out! God's mercy provides a way out if only we cry out to Him!

Have you reminded yourself recently about the deliverance His children have experienced in the past? He is still the same God who parted the Red Sea so the Israelites could escape the Egyptian army, the same God who delivered Daniel from the lions' den. And though we often pray for and desire to be delivered FROM our struggles and difficulties, sometimes He chooses to deliver us THROUGH them. Just as the refining process is used to remove impurities from a substance, God can use these seasons of trials to purify and grow His children, strengthening our faith in the process. There will also be a season of being delivered straight into His lov-

ing arms rather than being delivered from our struggles, unless we live to see Him return!

Often when others talk about aging and having
birthdays, they will comment that it is better than the
alternative. As I grow closer to God, I become more
homesick while living in a world that seems to grow
further away from Him. I say the alternative does not
look so bleak after all! As a matter of fact, being in His
presence for eternity sounds VERY AMAZING and
AWESOME to me. I look forward to the day when I can
see my Savior face-to-face and thank Him for all He has
done for me! That is the hope of believers and followers
of Jesus Christ!

Yet the loss of a loved one in this life is still so difficult. Life as we have known it changes, and change is
difficult. God's Word tells us there is a season for grief.
It also tells us that God will turn our mourning into
dancing! Don't fret! The light of the morning follows
the darkness of the night! But until the morning comes,
there are still glimpses of light in the darkness, just like
the stars and the moon in the night. And the darker the
night, the brighter those glimpses of light appear to
be. I call these grace moments! It is in those moments
when, though your heart is breaking in two, the God of
peace and joy is with you, and He is carrying you when
you need to be carried. Or maybe it is a physical suf-

fering, a financial burden that you are carrying. In surrendering our cares, whatever they may be, to God, He provides grace for the moment and reveals Himself in new and mighty ways!

Even while in an almost-constant state of loss, God provided all that was needed. While watching with concern as Kevin observed his daddy, whom he loved so much, declining, God provided all that was needed. When at the end, experiencing the physical loss of my dad, God provided all that was needed.

Thankfully, He also provided moments of joy to create more memories. My dad still had a spirit of determination about him, and he wanted to continue to do things as long as he could. He loved being with family, and he continued to host his family's Easter gathering each year. This was the tradition of his family to come together at Easter, and he wanted life to remain as normal as possible for Kevin as well as the rest of his family. He loved sports and went to ballgames as long as he possibly could, especially if Kevin wanted to go. He continued to have a garden, and when he could no longer do the work himself, he had someone else do it. But he enjoyed just going out and looking at the progress of growth. He could sit out there forever, or at least until he could no longer tolerate it.

I am extremely thankful to God that my dad never reached the point of not knowing who I was. I had felt all along that would be the saddest, most difficult thing about this illness. However, I know there are families who do reach that point. Some of those families are close to me or even extended family. I can't speak to what that would be like because I did not experience it. But it was what I dreaded most in relation to the illness after my dad's diagnosis. Maybe it was God's provision that my dad never got there. It's possible that for others, that would not be the most difficult part of this illness. I don't know. What I do know is that I trust that God would have provided grace needed for that, as well, had we experienced it.

I often wondered how aware my dad was of what the illness was doing to him. It appeared at times that he was not fully aware, but I was uncertain if it was due to a lack of acceptance or the illness. On one occasion, my dad was supposed to attend an anniversary reception for my aunt and uncle. He called another aunt the morning of the event and told her that he would be unable to attend. He told her that he did not know anything. He was cognizant of the fact that the reception was that day and he was supposed to attend because he called her to let her know he could not. But obviously he was able to sense a change occurring within him. Until this realization, I had always believed that this illness was much more difficult on the family than the individual with the illness.

Though watching a loved one suffer from dementia is difficult, I can't imagine being the one with the illness. But I saw God use the illness to answer prayers of concern regarding my dad. He appeared to find peace, which had long escaped him. This was evident in his relationships with others, and it was the answer to one of my two prayers I had prayed when he was diagnosed. I had prayed that he would find peace on earth before leaving and he did. In one strained relationship, he made a complete reversal in his care for this individual. In another, there was not as blatant of a change, but in discussions with him, it appeared evident that he had made peace in that situation, as well.

Though much loss was felt all along, God continued to answer prayers and provide for our needs. His grace sustained me physically, emotionally, and spiritually throughout my dad's illness. I cannot begin to imagine going through it without Him.

# 7

# Rapid Decline

Throughout the start of 2011, my father was rapidly declining, and by spring, he was not doing well at all. He was losing a lot of weight, and I had noticed that he was having difficulty feeding himself. Medication errors were becoming more frequent, and though he had moved another of my brothers in with him, this brother was not able to be responsible for the extent of care my dad needed. As I stated previously, he had his own impairment and was unable to care for himself, let alone someone with my dad's illness, which requires an intense level of care.

I was literally watching my dad wither away right before my eyes. Yet he insisted that this was the arrangement he wanted, and so we conceded for as long as possible. There were many struggles during this time, and I believe my dad endured things just to be able to continue the arrangement. I also believe his intent was to help my brother by keeping him there. He often stated he would have help in the home as long as it was an arrangement that was helping the caregiver. I am not sure he ever accepted that he was the one who needed the help.

However, he did comment to my aunt on one occasion that he might have to go to a nursing home as he was not getting the help he needed. He told her that Kevin was no longer helping him since my brother was there. Kevin told my aunt that my brother could do it. My brother needed extensive guidance to be the help my dad needed at this point in his illness. Due to my job, I just could not be there to provide that much guidance and support.

While they were there for Easter, my siblings and I did try talking to my brother who was living there. We hoped that this would help him realize the extent of support my dad needed. However, he was unable to carry that much responsibility, but I hoped he would recognize that and make a choice that would force my dad to seek additional help.

Some of my dad's specialists had begun to tell me they no longer needed to see him. They never explained why, and I recall taking my dad to his primary care physician on one occasion, but he saw the physician's assistant on that day. I told her about those who said they no longer needed to see him. I asked why and if they could see something that no one was telling me. She explained that some families do not want to discuss those things. I told her I was a planner, and I needed to know so I could be sure I was doing everything that needed to be done for him. She advised me to begin discussions with my dad about his wishes regarding feeding tubes and other medical decisions that would be needed.

My dad continued to decline, and during this time, a song entitled "Blessings" by Laura Story had been released, and I listened to this song constantly. It so helped put things into perspective. What an incredible blessing this song was to me. Often God's blessings do come out of our struggles and tears.

I recall on Father's Day in June 2011 realizing just how much more support my dad needed than he was getting and deciding it was time to get help in the home again. We had grilled at his home for him, preparing his favorite meal for Father's Day. As we sat at the table to eat with him, I realized that he was struggling tremendously to feed himself and was not likely getting the assistance he needed for meals. He had been losing weight, and I now knew the reason for the weight loss. I knew that due to my job I could not be there as much as was needed to ensure adequate nutrition.

After discussion about hiring someone, this time he was actually in agreement! Or at least he did not argue that he did not need the help! This time we hired

someone privately rather than going through an agen-
cy. We had a couple of different people until we could
find someone who was able to consistently help. What
a blessing she was! She had great experience and just
had a way with my dad that worked. This gave me peace
during the day, but he still was not getting the support
he needed at night and we were concerned he was not
eating anything for dinner.

He also began to appear to have difficulty swallowing. After discussion with his doctor, I took him for a
swallow study, and it was determined that he could
technically swallow but that he was forgetting or confused about the process (dementia as opposed to parkinsonism). His neurologist referred us to a specialist
for a consult for a feeding tube. I had previously discussed this with my dad, and he stated that if he ever
needed one, he wanted to have one. The specialist re-
viewed the results of the swallow study and stated that
my dad needed to wait until he could not swallow at all
before having the feeding tube put in.

Looking back, I believe my dad had already declined
in the area of swallowing since the study was done.
Maybe I should have insisted on the pursuit of the feeding tube. We look to the counsel of the professionals for
guidance, but remember, they are not the ones who are
living it! That does not mean that their counsel is not

needed. My dad's neurologist and his primary care physician were in agreement that if he wanted a feeding tube, it was time. I listened, however, to the counsel of this one physician who had only seen my dad once, and who had based his recommendation on a study that was likely outdated.

However, when you are in the midst of the decision-making, as things decline, it becomes so difficult to rely on your own instincts. It all becomes such an emotional roller coaster. However, I also know that God was still sovereign even in this, and His timing of the end of my dad's life on this earth was still in His hands...feeding tube or no feeding tube.

The Holy Spirit provides counsel and guidance, so trust in God's wisdom and understanding for the decisions for your loved one and your family. His Word tells us to *"Trust the LORD with all your heart and do not lean on your own understanding"* (Prov. 3:5 NASB). But He does not leave us there without an understanding to trust in. God is the source of true wisdom and understanding, as is stated in 1 Chronicles 22:12: *"Only the LORD give you discretion and understanding..."* (NASB).

My dad continued to decline, and he spent the last ten days of June 2011 in the hospital due to renal failure. He was experiencing a lack of nutrition and hydration, as well as medication errors. These could likely have contributed to the renal failure. He had also begun to have chronic pneumonia and urinary tract infections.

He went to rehab from the hospital in hopes of strengthening physically prior to returning home. However, he was only in rehab one day before returning to the hospital for pneumonia and a urinary tract infection. He was in the hospital ten more days, which were the first ten days of July 2011. While he was in the hospital this time, I questioned whether he would be going home...at least to his earthly home. There were just moments when I knew he would not be with us much longer. My oldest son, Joshua, was getting married in August of that year, so during this time, I also had many wedding events and much planning going on. Though I am very much a planner, I can often be a procrastinator with the follow-through. However, by an absolute miracle of God, I had all of my plans for the rehearsal dinner made early, as well as all purchases that could be made this far in advance. All this was done prior to my father's first visit to the hospital. God was truly looking out for me!

I recall on one occasion being with my dad at the hospital in July, and he seemed to be growing worse. My sister came for a visit, and while there, she stayed with Dad so that I could leave the hospital. I walked to my car and got in and closed the door. As I had sensed that he might not be going back to his earthly home after this hospital visit, I prayed, "Lord, I know Your timing is perfect, but please remember I am getting ready for a wedding." In that moment, He reminded me that He is preparing for a wedding, as well, and I sensed Him ask, "Are you truly, fully, completely Mine?" I sensed I was soon to be at a crossroads if I was not already.

Once home, I needed to do a few things on the computer. While I was on the computer, I noticed that Casting Crowns was previewing another song from their new CD that was to be released soon. What amazing timing my Lord had and still has. The preview was for "Wedding Day." I listened to the song continuously that day. Yes...someday this suffering will end, and He will wipe away all our tears! There will be no more pain or death! There will be no more grief or sorrow! All who thirst will be satisfied! All things will be made new and beautiful and full of life! We will dwell forever in the presence of the God of love! We will look into the face of Jesus and experience what now is only imagined! There will be no more night and our light will be the glory of God! All who love the Lord above all and have been cleansed will enter the gates! What hope and sweet victory is found in that message! (Rev. 21–22).

Ahhhhhh! That just speaks such hope to my soul. Amazingly, though I am not a choreographer...and not really a dancer, I still have a dance in my head to that song that God placed there that day! I do have music in my head most of the time, though, so I guess a dance was sure to happen eventually! What a tough summer, with the roller coaster of emotions between my dad's decline and my son's wedding. And God was providing me with a song of hope AND a dance! Now, that is surely the joy of the Lord in action!

My dad was released again to a rehabilitation facility, and he was there over the next few weeks. Various family members would receive phone calls from him stating that they (the rehab workers, not his family) were starving him to death, and he would request food. I think he just did not like the food, and he also wanted...hoped for...someone to come get him. After a few weeks, he also had peaked as far as he could go in therapy. During a staffing session, I was told that they did not feel he would make any further progress and he would need to be released. He went home in August.

He was able to be at my son's wedding in August, but he was not doing well. We were so thankful that he was able to be there regardless. It meant so much to me, because I did not have a big wedding and he was not there for it. I had no idea how much this bothered him until my twenty-fifth wedding anniversary, when my dad suggested that we have a ceremony to renew our vows and have our family there. He expressed how much he wished he had been at our wedding. I declined the renewal of vows because our anniversary was just a couple of months after my father-in-law had passed, and I thought it would be too difficult for that side of the family.

I knew in my heart that Joshua's wedding would be our last family photo with my dad. I wanted to make sure we got a photo with all my siblings in addition to a photo with my family. Though the photos are very revealing of the decline he had experienced, I am still grateful for them.

He did remain stable until September 1, 2011, and on that date, I had to take him to the emergency room. Not only did God allow me time for the wedding, but He also gave me a few days of rest prior to the final downhill plunge. His grace is truly sufficient. I recall just beginning to feel rested the last day of August after the wedding, and there were no emergencies or medical issues until the first day of September, at which time, he was in the emergency room. I was not provided much information by the ER doctor, and he sent my dad home.

On September 2, 2011, my dad was scheduled to have a procedure for the replacement of his pacemaker. The life of the battery/generator—whatever the correct terminology—was concluding. We went to an appointment for pre-op with the surgeon following my dad's emergency room visit. Based on labs from the emergency room visit, we were told he would have to get his potassium levels and INR levels back in range or he would not be able to have this surgery. The surgeon actually appeared alarmed that he had not been admitted to the hospital at the time of the emergency room visit.

I stayed with my dad at his home that evening to give him the foods that would aid in reaching those goals. He was served (and fed) sauerkraut and turnip greens for dinner. What an enticing meal! He loves both foods, but to have nothing but those foods, as well as those in combination, did not appeal to me. I feared that if I gave him anything else, though, I would not be able to get enough of those in him to impact the levels.

We went in for the surgery, and blood was drawn to determine if the procedure could be done, and we had been successful! All levels were where they needed to be, and he went in for surgery. Afterward he went back home, and he continued to have private care in the mornings through lunch.

# 8

# Answered Prayer

During the month of September 2011, I felt drawn to purchase an accompaniment compact disc for a song. I knew in my heart that I was preparing to sing this song at my dad's funeral, but I did not allow my mind to go there. I took time for shopping, which had been a very rare thing over the past few years, going out of town to a Christian bookstore. I had already picked up the accompaniment track, and I continued to browse in the store.

While in the bookstore, I felt very drawn to a book. I tried to talk myself out of it...I just did not feel I had time to read right now....I had not gone there for a book...all the rational explanations. But the book just kept jumping out at me! I do not know if that has ever happened to you, but I have learned that when God wants to show me something, He can be very persistent! If it continues to jump, I take notice! I thank Him that He does not quit trying with me when I do not listen the first time.

The title of the book was *Heaven Is for Real* by Todd
Burpo with Lynn Vincent. [1] If you are not familiar with
the book, it is about a small child who during a very serious illness visits heaven. It is not fiction, but it is the
father's account of the actual experience as reported by
his son. I finally succumbed to the strong internal urging that I was to read this book. I made my purchase
and left to go home.

When I got home, I decided to take a look at the book
and maybe read a few pages. However, I could not put
the book down, and I completed it that same night! In
this book, a grandson sees his great-grandfather, whom
he had never met, in heaven. The significance of this is
that his father had heard his mother cry at times over
concerns that her father might not have gone to heaven
because he did not speak of spiritual things. God had
just revealed to me that though my dad might not speak
of spiritual things, he would, in fact, be in heaven! That
might not seem to be a definitive acknowledgment of
that fact to you. But it is one of those things that I cannot explain, but just had to experience!

This was the second and final prayer I had prayed
when my dad was initially diagnosed, and it had been
answered! I was also reminded of my dad's care and
concern for the widows and the fatherless. He was very

1  Burpo, Todd, Heaven is for Real, (Nashville, Thomas Nelson,
2010).

generous to those in need, which spoke volumes about his heart. This was also confirmation to me. Little did I know that God was yet to provide further confirmation that my dad would be in heaven! He is soooooooo good!

My dad continued to decline, and during September, it became apparent that he needed a greater level of care 24/7, and he probably should have had it months ago. The decision of what to do was a very emotional and difficult process. My dad never wanted to have to come to my home, and I wanted to honor that wish if I could. But I honestly did not want him to go to a long-term care facility. I checked into personal care homes and found a possible home. After some discussion, I made the decision to take him there.

He said he would stay if I stayed with him. That was heart-wrenching for me. However, I left him there one night and once I was home, I was unable to sleep. I would go to bed and start crying. Dennis was still up, and I would go to him and discuss my concerns about leaving him there. I went back to bed and started crying again. I got up and went to Dennis again, discussing my concerns. I went back to bed and started crying again. I went to Dennis and asked, "You said he could come here, right?" He reaffirmed that we could bring him to our home, and so the decision was made to contact the personal care home owner the following morning and discuss his release. I was immediately able to go to sleep. I had such peace, which confirmed for me that this was the right decision.

The following morning, I confirmed that the help we had hired for him in his home would also come to our home during the day when we were working. I then called the owner of the personal care home and discussed bringing him home, and an agreement was made for him to leave. I had total peace once he was at my home, and I fully believe that this was confirmation that we had made the right decision for us. As I said previously, family dynamics are different, and this does not work for everyone. However, in addition to the feeling of peace and ability to sleep, there were other moments that confirmed this as the right decision for us. Again, I tried to include my siblings in as many decisions as possible, but the reality is that unless you are the one providing care, you may not be able to realize the right decision for your home and family. Nor can you decide for someone else whether they can manage caring for someone in their home.

I realized later that I had some special moments with my dad that I likely would have missed had he been somewhere else. There were moments of clarity when he could engage in conversation. I realize that if he had been somewhere else and I was just in and out checking on him, I likely would have missed a lot of those moments. There were moments of doing things for him that we knew he loved, such as taking him outside, that he might not have been able to do there. On one occasion, we took him outside for a while and sat with him. When we needed to go inside to prepare dinner, we asked if he was ready to go in, and he stated he wanted to remain outside. Dennis moved his wheelchair to a place where we could see him from the doorway and let him remain out there for a while longer. Dennis had him wave to my brother and sister and took a picture to send to them.

During the last few days my dad spent at my home just prior to going into the hospital the final time, he became very weak. His voice was so soft he was barely audible, and his eyes were barely open. He loved being outdoors, so we continued to take him out in his wheelchair so he could just sit and enjoy the fresh air and creation. We also tried to move him from different chairs and positions to prevent any skin issues as he was not walking at all at this point.

On one occasion, he was sitting in his wheelchair facing the television. He made a comment that made me question if he might be in another time period of his life, so I asked him where he was. He replied that he was in Chicago. Not quite sure how to respond to that, I asked him how he got there. He did not respond. I then asked him if he knew who I was. He said he believed so and called my name. Another minute or so passed, and he suddenly turned his head toward me with his eyes WIDE open and STRENGTH and CONVICTION in his voice and said, "The good Lord is watching over you!" I was speechless! It was obvious he had seen or heard something that I could not. What a gift...what a blessing...what an amazing God! Did my dad make a visit to heaven and pass over Chicago on the way up?! I cannot understand the details of what happened, but one day I will! All I know is that God gave me reassurance through my dad in spite of dementia! Take that, enemy of God! God also further confirmed my dad's connection to Him and assured me that he would be in heaven! It was further confirmation of God's answer to that prayer!

I have to interject here a passage of scripture that has come to life for me in recent months. Ephesians 3:10 states, *"So that the manifold wisdom of God might now be made known through the church to the rulers and authorities in the heavenly places"* (NASB). In previous verses, Paul stated that he was the recipient of grace through the revelation of the gospel. He states that God's revelation to him was for the purpose of sharing the gospel with the Gentiles and to reveal the unity of Jews and Gentiles in Christ.

Now, we all tend to, at times, get caught up in the difficulties of life and think it is all about us! However, this verse would be contradictory to that line of thought. My initial reaction to this verse was, Whoa... that makes me want to take much more seriously the transforming and renewing of my mind so that all my words and actions would be a revelation of God's wisdom rather than my weakness.

But I believe that God reveals His wisdom through the Church to the principalities and powers by what His Spirit does in and through us in spite of our weakness! His Word tells us that it is in our weakness that He is strong. Have you ever observed a cracked pot or lantern with a candle or light in it? Or a door that does not quite fit the framework with a light on behind the closed door? It is through the cracks that you will see the light! Those weak areas of the pot, lantern, or doorway yield way to the light within! I am definitely a cracked pot! It is in those weak areas where God really "shines"! His power at work in us reveals Himself to others when we allow Him to do works that others can see and know that it had to be the one true God.

In the third chapter of Daniel, Shadrach, Meshach, and Abed-Nego were thrown into a fiery furnace for

refusing to worship a statue that King Nebuchadnezzar had ordered to be erected. When Nebuchadnezzar
saw four men in the furnace rather than three, he knew
and declared it was the Son of God. He acknowledged
the God of Shadrach, Meshach, and Abed-Nego and ordered that no one say anything against their God (see
Dan. 3:29). We serve the same God, and He can reveal
Himself to others through us. It is sometimes our walk
during storms or through the fire that He uses to do
this.

What grace God provided during my dad's illness,
and as difficult as caregiving is, I never lost hope. I almost never lost peace, which after briefly lost was re-
stored when I surrendered my dad's care to God rather
than me. Though I had sad moments, I never lost the
joy of the Lord. When I had no strength to continue,
God carried me. When I was hurt by words of agitation
due to the illness, God healed my heart and sheltered
me. When there were difficult decisions to make, God
provided wisdom and understanding. Even as my dad
declined, there were so many grace moments that cannot be explained, only experienced.

During my dad's illness, the Lord had given me an
additional chorus to a song but He just recently provided the verses. This is a song of hope for all seasons
of life.

## Chorus
*Jesus, redeemer of my life.*
*Jesus, healer of my heart.*
*Jesus, lover of my soul.*
*Jesus, the One who saved me.*
*Jesus, the One who raised me.*
*Jesus, the One who makes me whole.*

## Verse 1
*In a dark and lonely place,*
*broken and afraid.*
*Jesus came and rescued me.*
*Praise His holy name.*

## Verse 2
*When the road seems hard and long,*
*and you can't go on,*
*just cry out Jesus' name.*
*To you, He's holding on.*

## Bridge
*Power...in His name.*
*Freedom...in His name.*
*Victory...in His name.*
*King of kings and Lord of lords.*
*Praise His holy name.*

God never promised us that this life would be easy or without suffering. He did promise, however, that we would never have to walk alone. His presence is always with us, no matter how alone we feel. Regardless of the darkness we are surrounded by, His light can pierce the darkness. If we can only know and understand who He is and the depth of His love for us, we can face difficulties with peace and joy, which only comes from knowing Him. And when your struggle has you so encumbered that you are unsure how you should pray, just call out the name of Jesus. There IS power, freedom, and victory in His name...the name above all names!

# 9

# Ultimate Victory

My dad spent his last ten days in the hospital with pneumonia and developing sepsis. I had believed that he was aspirating due to holding food in his mouth, and finally during this time in the hospital a nurse concurred with me. The doctor stated he was too malnourished to fight off the infection. The last few days he spent in intensive care.

I called my sister, and she made arrangements to come be with him, as well. In talking with her on the day following this discussion of plans, she debated waiting a day later to come. I believed that she did not need to wait so I just politely informed her that my dad was expecting her on the original date planned because I had already told him she was coming. She agreed to come as planned. My brother was there also, and we planned to take turns at night being at the hospital. However, once my dad saw my sister, he made his journey home early the following morning. I believe he was waiting to see her because I had told him that she was coming.

My dad had no more pain...no more sadness...no more confusion...no more tremors...no more hunger... no more thirst...and he was for eternity fully mobile. He was experiencing victory over death, and he was in the presence of the One who provided that victory through His own death and resurrection! He had left the pain and suffering of this world behind, and he was now in a place that I can only imagine. Physical disease had served as a conduit, by which his soul had been urged on to his real, eternal home. What was meant by the enemy for bad, was in fact victory for my dad!

It had been almost six years from the time my dad was diagnosed until he made his final journey to his heavenly home. In the midst of the six years, it seemed to last an eternity. But of my dad's seventy-four years, it was just a season. Of my fifty-one years (at the time), it was but a season. We go through periods of trial and suffering in this life, but praise God they are temporary! Thank You, Lord, for the promise of eternity with You...in Your presence...in continuous praise and worship of and service to our Creator who longs to be with us! Oh, to comprehend the height, depth, breadth, and width of His love!

Since the loss of my dad, his sister suffered with a similar, if not the same illness. She is now experiencing full healing in the presence of the Lord. And, oh my, what a reunion I am sure they had. And in the midst of their illnesses there has been hope...a peace that passes all understanding. And when God chose to deliver her by the fire into His presence, her faith was then perfected!

We often question where God is in times of pain and suffering and how He can allow it. I can assure you, He is right there with you. We live in a fallen, imperfect world, which results in suffering. But God did not create you and provide salvation through the death of His Son just to leave you out here on your own! He cares, and He loves you so very much. He shelters us beneath His wings. And when we feel we are weary and have no strength to carry on...He carries us! And when we are in need...He provides for us! And when we have questions...He gives wisdom and understanding! And when life's demands are overwhelming and beyond our capacity of responsibility...He is sovereign! And when we are at risk...He protects us! And when we feel that we are lost in time...He reassures us! And He is preparing for the wedding of all weddings! Hallelujah, hallelujah, hallelujah, and amen!

*Then I heard something like the voice of a great multitude and like the sound of many waters and like mighty peals of thunder, saying: "Halle-*

*lujah! For the Lord our God, the Almighty, reigns.
Let us rejoice and be glad and give the glory to
Him, for the marriage of the Lamb has come, and
His bride has made herself ready."*
—Revelation 19:6–7 NASB

# Epilogue

Eight and a half years have passed since my dad left this earth. There are very few days that go by that I do not think of him. However, the sweet memories have become more prevalent than the sad memories.

Life continues, and Kevin has continued to live in his home with support. We have continued the Easter celebrations at my dad's home with his family. It is different without him there, but I know his celebration with the Savior, without whom we would have no reason to celebrate, is so sweet. I cannot wish him to be here, though I do miss him.

I miss that he planted raspberries because he knew I liked them. I miss that he planted a vegetable garden so all those he cared about could benefit from it, even if he was unable to harvest and cook. I miss that he could answer so many questions for me. I miss his laugh and his smile and occasionally his prankster ways! I miss his competitive spirit with my boys regarding their height and shoe size! I miss grilling salmon and vegetables and making homemade cherry ice cream for him because he loved it so much, which was a love I shared with him. I miss him being at his home for Easter when we have our family gatherings, which we have continued. I miss that we shared such a love for watermelon!

Yes...the sadness has dissipated. But I still miss him. But I would not wish him back here for anything in this world. He suffered greatly in this life, as we all do. He has now experienced complete victory over suffering, and he no longer experiences pain or sorrow. And if you know Jesus...not just know about Him...but truly know Him as your Lord and Savior...someday...just someday...that sweet victory will be yours, as well!

I pray that you do know Him. The height, depth, breadth, and width of His love for you cannot be measured! It cannot be contained in a tomb! The light of His love cannot be concealed in the midst of darkness! His glory shines in our midst, and He is everywhere...in the majesty of the mountains...the beauty of the waterfalls... the song of the birds...the vastness of the oceans...and yes, even in the midst of suffering! God is all around us! Know Him...bask in His love...find redemption in His mercies...rest in His grace...find shelter in His arms... and may His peace that passes all understanding sustain you in the struggles and sorrow, as well as in the happy moments of this life.

*Now to the King eternal, immortal, invisible, the only God, be honor and glory forever and ever. Amen.*
— 1 Timothy 1:17 NASB

DIANE BENTLEY